CUBEONOMICS

How smart women get
beyond their cubes,
build strategic relationships
and boost their brand

By Karyn Quick

Copyright © 2018 by Karyn Quick

All content is copyrighted, and all rights are reserved. This book or any portion thereof may not be reproduced or used in any manner whatsoever without the express written permission from the publisher.

Table of Contents

ACKNOWLEDGEMENTS 4

INTRODUCTION: OWN YOUR POWER 6

MY FRUSTRATING STORY 13

LANDING THE PROMOTION 19

CHAPTER 1: BREAK MENTAL BARRIERS 30

    FEAR 31
    PROCRASTINATION 35
    PERCEIVED LACK OF KNOWLEDGE, ... 43
    EFFECTIVE COMMUNICATION 49
    EMOTIONAL INTELLIGENCE 53

CHAPTER 2: RAISE YOUR VISIBILITY 56

CHAPTER 3: BOOST YOUR BRAND 70

CHAPTER 4: CONNECTION IS COLLECTION: 77

CHAPTER 5: GET STARTED: LIFE IS WAITING 86

CONCLUSION 95

Acknowledgements

I'd like to say thank you to my loving mother Gloria Quick for your support and raising me to be the strong, independent, successful woman I am today.

To my dad, Sylvester Jackson, thank you for inspiring me to consider entrepreneurship. I watched as you worked and built your successful business.

To my coach Jonathan Sprinkles, thank you for your guidance and support in helping me bring my vision to life so I could birth my dream.

To the focus group contributors:
1. Anissa Zabriskie, CPC, MBA
2. Bendedra Allen-Welch
3. Catina Edmond, MPA
4. Karen Jones, MBA, PMP

5. Leanna Land
6. L. Nicole Cervantes, M.S.W
7. Ranada Rainey-Reese, M. Ed.
8. Rosalind Walker-Lewis, MBA
9. Shelley Davis Jones, Ed.D.
10. Tandee Salter

Thank you for coming alongside me sharing your knowledge, insight and support in a non-judgmental way. Your team spirit provided the necessary support that allowed me to include information in this book that will help some career women avoid some of the challenges we faced in our careers.

Introduction: Own Your Power

Women are powerful! Women earn 60% of the Bachelor and Master's Degrees in this country. Women account for 47% of the US Labor force and 50.8% of the US Population. Women hold 52% of all professional jobs. Women make up the majority of the US population, yet women still lag behind our male counterparts in holding only 25% of leadership roles and in Corporate America the numbers a slightly lower at 18% according to Center for American Progress.

I know you're probably asking yourself, what is Cubeonomics? Well, I am glad you asked. Cubeonomics is the economics behind why it's essential for smart women to get beyond their cubes, build strategic relationships and boost their brands to add value to valuable people.

Ladies, we can no longer afford to allow ourselves to stay confined in our mind, body and actions. We deserve to be appreciated and rewarded for the value and commitment that we bring to an organization.

Are you fed up with feeling stuck in your career? Are you tired of working in a mundane or un-fulfilling job? Are you tired of being overlooked for that raise? Are you tired of working nights and weekends hoping you get the visibility? Are you sick and tired of seeing your male counterparts being promoted over you? If you answered yes to any of these questions, then you're not alone. There are countless women who have been or are still where you are, and we know exactly how you feel.

This book will teach some ground-breaking, what I call "secret side door" information that will transform and change the trajectory of your career and life. Yes, I said change your life, and I know you're asking yourself, why is she saying life—isn't this is a career book?

I say change your life because statistics have shown that women tend to blend their career and personal lives and if they are not satisfied in their career then they are not satisfied in their personal life. For example, when things at work are not going well, you start to second guess all your accomplishments: the degree or certification you received, whether you're worthy, whether it's your fault and if you did something to cause things to be the way they are. I am here to tell you that if you doubt yourself in any way, stop it, it's not your fault and I am here to help.

What this book will not be covering is the traditional linear approach to elevating your career. This mode of operation is ingrained into our very being, so we have mastered it. We have always been taught work hard, stay in your cube, keep your head down and appear like you're being busy and productive. This was supposed to get us noticed by the promotion angels up in the stratosphere, and we should miraculously receive the recognition, raise and promotion. I am here to tell you this approach alone does not work and will not get you the desired results you want to move forward in your career.

In this book, I am not encouraging you to step away from your cube, cubicle, desk or however you prefer to name the location where you perform your job and neglect getting your work done. That is the last thing I am implying here; you must work hard and be great at what you do; that is first and foremost. If your work performance is not up to par, then you don't have time to invest in the strategies I am going to share with you in this book. You see, you were hired for your specific skill set and the value you bring to the organization, so you must perform. Of course, you want to keep your job, your commitment to your employer and a paycheck.

The message I will convey in this book is that performing your job well is not enough to get you to the next level in your career.

What we know for sure is women are still feeling stuck and dissatisfied with their jobs and they're not getting the exposure and opportunities like their male counterparts.

We hear the talk, but the numbers are not changing. We hear the talk, but according to the results in the Census Bureau, women are still only making eighty cents to every dollar earned by their male counterparts performing the same jobs.

It's time we ask ourselves why things are not changing for women; the conversations are happening, books are being written, but the numbers are not changing.

In my research, I found that the information available is hard to follow, contain very few practical action steps and the steps provided are cumbersome and cannot be quickly implemented.

Then there is some information asking women to conform to be someone that they are not, challenging their integrity and not aligning with their core values and beliefs.

In today's society, there are competing demands on our time, and its essential information is disseminated where we can see ourselves taking the actions quickly. Information must be packaged where big chunks can be broken down into bite-size actionable pieces that can be easily implemented and give us that quick win.

The strategies I will share in this book have allowed me and my clients to have rewarding careers that most people dream about having. The experiences I have been blessed to have, have helped me grow into the confident, successful, culturally aware and humble woman that I am today. Let me share with you a little about myself and my journey because if you know me, you can hear me and what I have to share with you in this book.

My Frustrating Story

I am a Global Tech Leader who manages and develops global leaders in various countries: US, Brazil, Europe, India, Netherlands, and Singapore. I have travelled and worked in four of the seven continents, so that leaves only three more to go. I have earned two degrees: my Bachelor of Computer Science and a Master's in Business. Currently I hold the role of President for the local chapter of my sorority. I live by the mantra, "To whom much is given, much is required," so I spend countless hours serving and touching the lives of many residents in my local communities.

It may look like I have had a privileged life and that the road I travelled was paved with gold. I am here to let you know that is far from the truth. Building my career has not been as easy as it may appear from the outside looking in.

What you don't know about me is it hasn't always been this way. My life has been much like our friends in the movie Wizard of Oz; you remember all the challenges Dorothy with the glass slippers, and her group of friends faced as they travelled on the yellow brick road to Oz? Much like this group, I too went down a very similar yellow brick road and, on my journey, there were many twists and turns which I refer to as challenges or opportunities. And yes, at times, they were frustrating.

I have had many mountains to climb, bruised knees from falling in potholes, rivers to cross with high seas and disappointments to bounce back from after being bumped against many walls.

I hope I have painted the picture for you that life for me has not been comfortable as it may seem and like many of you, I have been stuck in my career many, many, many times. I am sure, I missed some many's, but you get the point.

The first challenge thrust upon me early in my career was working in the male-dominated field of Information Technology (IT). I was the only woman attending the meetings for the projects I supported, and I was in the boardroom with all alpha males. As you can imagine, this was very intimidating for a young professional just starting off in her career.

The men I worked around were very traditional, and they would rarely listen to me and they did not seem to value any

information I shared in the meetings. I didn't
think they were valuing the information until
they would regurgitate the same points I made
in the meeting and use them as their own to
make a point. They would talk over me to get
their points across and would never circle
back to me on any of the discussions.

I realized that even when they didn't say it,
they showed me through their actions that
they expected me to conform with their
decisions. As I sat in the meetings with these
powerful personalities, I could see my 5' 9"
body shrinking to the size of a child right
before my eyes. Growing up in an inner-city
community also known as "The Hood,"
where others around me were having children,
getting involved in gangs and selling drugs, I
stood on my confidence, persevered and
pushed through to make it out of that
environment. Where was this drive,

confidence and assurance that helped me beat the odds and escape without being another statistic? I have always been a very confident woman but put into this situation with no guidance on how to navigate, made me feel inferior, unsure and challenged the confidence I built within.

I lost my confidence in those meetings where I so needed to stand up against my male co-workers; instead I shrank and dimmed my light, so they would not feel insecure or intimidated by my presence. I needed them to know, like, and trust me for them to work with me so that I could get the information needed from them to be successful.

This strategy was effective yet ineffective; it allowed me to fit in, but it came with a cost; the cost of me feeling empty inside, unfulfilled, confined and darn stuck. It was as if my inner-self was sinking in quicksand with no way out.

This mode of operation was a disservice to my self-esteem and my professional growth and development. It was not a win/win situation like they talk about in the Corporate world.

As I reflect on the situation, it boiled down to me not having the confidence and certainty to take risks and stand up for myself no matter what. I was stuck with my two best friends, "Stagnate and Complacency," and it took me eight years before I received my first promotion into a leadership role.

Landing the Promotion

It was a Friday. I remember it like it was yesterday when a friend of mine in management dropped by my cube and informed me that he had thrown my name in the hat for a new position that was available. I had worked with him on various projects and he knew my work and thought this position, although it was a lateral move, would be an excellent opportunity for my career.

I sat on his suggestion and thought about it over the weekend. The self-doubt angel visited me, rested on my shoulder and whispered in my ear all the reasons why I should not go for the position. It was the fear of the unknown and stepping into uncharted territory because this would be a brand-new organization for the company. After much thought, hot sweats and sleepless nights, I mustered up the confidence to step outside my box, the safe place I had created for myself, I applied and interviewed for this new position.

I was successful in my efforts and received the position under a new manager. Although the position was a lateral move, this opportunity allowed me to expand my skillset.

To my surprise, what I didn't know was that I was gaining a manager who saw more in me than I had seen in myself because I was still dealing with a lot of the self-doubt and unworthy baggage I obtained working with my previous team. This manager poured into me by helping me strengthen my leadership skills, navigate corporate politics, reduce my confusion and uncertainty related to company culture, and jump-started my networking which helped me learn how to connect with valuable people.

I had no idea what she was preparing me for, but I was soaking it up like a sponge, applying the knowledge and the next year I was promoted into my first leadership role. I didn't put all my energy focusing on getting a promotion; instead, I focused on learning and executing the strategies that would position me to get the higher position. I felt as if my career was finally moving in the right direction and there was light at the end of the tunnel.

I now look back and know it was the calm before the storm, you know the feeling of driving on a warm summer day with the windows down, wind blowing through your hair and you don't have a care in the world; that is how I felt working under my new manager.

Then the terrible storm hit, the market shifted, and the company underwent a significant downsizing. During this transition, Although I was not laid off I watch my colleagues walking out with their boxes through seven very daunting, draining and depressing layoffs.

As I dreaded, due to the realignment of the organization, I now worked for a new manager. At this point, I had been leading multiple teams for several years and had an excellent track record with performance reviews to co-sign for my success.

I give you this background not to boast or brag but to set the tone for the next significant hurdles I would have to overcome in my career. Under this new manager, working hard was an understatement. I found myself working ten times harder than I had ever worked, leading teams in three different time zones only to continue to get the same standard 3% raise year after year with no promotion in sight.

During the annual appraisal, I was seeing my male co-workers promoted while I was still wearing the annual poker face, confused about why my career was at a standstill. I was doing what traditionally we were taught to do: working hard, working crazy hours and starting all over again the next day. My work and responsibilities were steadily increasing but what was not showing up was the money or higher position for my contributions. Have you ever been overlooked for a promotion? Have you been slighted on your raises? Have you ever felt stuck in your career? If you answered yes to any of these questions, you're not alone. This is precisely how I felt for several years in my career.

I made a pact with myself that it was time to step out on faith in the next meeting with my boss. I would communicate and highlight all my documented accomplishments and ask for that raise and promotion. The big day came, and I was ready to execute my plan; I practiced my speech along with all supporting facts over and over to ensure I was prepared.

As I sat down at the table in the meeting, my manager informed me they put me on the non-promotable list. It felt like I received a swift punch in my gut; I was not aware this list existed, so I questioned its purpose. He gave me a vague excuse about it being something new the company was exploring, and it didn't mean I couldn't be promoted. I looked at him in amazement that he would insult my intelligence. It doesn't take a rocket scientist to know if you're being placed on a non-promotable list, you're probably not going to be promoted.

I found myself stuck once again in my career, thinking thoughts of self-doubt, unworthiness and self-pity creeping back and challenging my very being due to being placed on this non-promotable list. But you know what they say, when it rains, it pours. Just when I thought nothing else could happen the ultimate did.

My director walked into my cube and informed me that he had hired this lady, placed her on my team, told me to make her successful, and never mind the fact she had no IT experience. She was a thorn in my side from day one; it was as if she knew she had favor with my director and used it to her advantage. She sought out to make my job a living hell and eventually convinced my director to put me on a Performance Improvement Plan (PIP). These plans are like death sentences to your career, and you rarely heard where someone had successfully completed them. The norm was most people lost their jobs in the process. I knew my performance did not warrant me being placed on this plan.

I felt disrespected and betrayed. For a moment I started to wallow in my sorrow because it sent me back to the time in my career when I felt hopeless, unworthy and less than my colleagues, I knew I never wanted to revisit that place, so I lay in self-pity for a minute then I dusted myself off and I exercised many of the skills I had learned from my prior Boss and mentors. These skills allowed me to fight this PIP so I fought for several months until I gained the support of the VP of HR to get the "PIP" dropped. I prevailed against what I thought initially was the end of the road for me and my career.

These challenges although very daunting, draining and time consuming, taught me some key lessons that have shaped the trajectory of how my career is today. I spent countless hours doing some self-evaluation and soul searching to gain an understanding of what was in my control where I could have had some influence on the outcome to make the result in these situations different. I didn't allow myself to focus on the elements of these situations I could not control. Due to this ordeal, I learned to be visible, strategically align myself with the right connections, be prepared and have the appropriate tools to leverage.

The toolkit should not only contain the written rules but also the strategies for the unwritten rules that are also needed to navigate and steer your career in the direction that will serve you most.

The lessons that I learned as a result of being stuck in my career lead me to develop a system I call "The Quick 6"; the strategies that are a part of my proven success system allows women to get unstuck and get the raise or promotion they deserve.

What women are missing are the strategies built into this system. This system works, and it works quickly and that is why it is called, "The Quick 6"; why some women are still stuck is because they are doing one or a few but nobody is doing all six, and that's why the numbers are not changing.

In this book, I will be sharing the first strategy of "The Quick 6" called "Cubeonomics". The other five strategies of this system will be forthcoming in future books.

In Cubeonomics, I address four core areas that will help you gain a competitive edge and catapult you to the next level in your career:

1) Breaking Mental Barriers
2) Gaining Visibility
3) Building Strategic Relationships
4) Boosting Your Brand

Chapter 1: Break Mental Barriers

Women! Shift from thinking, "I'm not ready to do that," to thinking "I will, I must, I shall do that, and I will learn by taking action."
—Karyn Quick

Our thoughts have power, so we must be careful what we allow to take up real estate in our minds. The first step to invoking change is recognizing there is a paradigm shift we need to make in how we think. The problem lies in what we feed our mind which keeps us in mental bondage. Shifting our thinking is the first step in creating an amazing reality for ourselves. The way we think is a direct correlation to the way our lives unfold. Protect your thinking like you protect your money, your children and the thing you love with all your heart and soul.

In the spirit of recognizing and protecting our thinking let me start by exposing some of the top mental barriers that kept me, my clients, and you feeling stuck, stifled, dissatisfied and/or frustrated with the way things are for you in your life.

The areas I will address are:
1) Fear
2) Procrastination
3) Perceived lack of Knowledge
4) Effective Communication
5) Emotional Intelligence

Fear is one of the most detrimental mental barriers that keep us feeling stuck. Statistics show that 90% of successful people have allowed fear to keep them from moving forward in various aspects of their lives. Fear is genuine, but we must learn how to leverage its power to propel us forward versus allowing it to hold us back. Oprah Winfrey stated it best, "What we fear most has no Power, it is your fear that has the Power." We spend valuable time pondering: what if this happens, what if that happens, to where we lose sight of our goals and never act.

We have allowed fear to rob us of our dreams and aspirations for far too long. Although, life bring forth challenges. Statistics show that 85% of what we fear will never happen to us in our lifetime. The other 15% of what we worry about happens, but usually it's things we can manage and that will never destroy us but will teach us a lesson that we can pack in our success toolkit to help us as we deal with future challenges. It is liberating and empowering to know that there are learnings in our successes and greater learning in our failures. Winston Churchill says, "Success is stumbling from failure to failure with no loss of enthusiasm."

In my career, I used to always want things to be 100% correct and never wanted to make a mistake or be viewed as someone who didn't have the answers to solve whatever problem arose. This was the farthest from the truth; I didn't have all the answers, but I was good at camouflaging the fact that I didn't have all the answers. I feared if I appeared as if I didn't have the answer or if I asked too many probing questions it would send a signal that I didn't know my job and I would be viewed as a fraud which would result in a lousy performance review. Our performance reviews are viewed as the blueprint for our careers and we protect them at all costs. Due to this fear, I did what most people who feared bad reviews did, put on a happy face and faked it. This behavior that was a result of fear didn't allow me to grow as quickly as I could have if I would have stood up to the fear and asked the questions that would allow me to learn and grow. I was stuck in my career in a non-leadership role for eight years afraid of asking for a raise or promotion because I had several fears:

1. Fear of leaving my friends behind and not being liked
2. Fear of the haters (i.e. Jealous Colleagues) that could try to sabotage my success
3. Fear of the unknown on the other side of success
4. Fear of the what would be expected of me once I attained the next level.

It was much safer for me to continue doing what I was doing because I was making a decent salary and 60% of my efforts were some of my colleagues 100%, so compared to them I was doing darn good. You see fear weakened and crippled my mind, it had me comparing myself to other people to validate my decision to stay stuck, and it didn't allow for me to move forward which left me feeling stifled, unworthy and agitated because I wanted more but didn't have the guts to go and get it. Jack Canfield said it best, "Everything you want is on the other side of Fear."

Procrastination presents itself when you delay or postpone things you should get done now for a future time. It also shows up when that voice in your head start giving you excuse after excuse after excuse, giving yourself permission not to move forward.

Think of the times you told yourself, "I'll do it later," "I'll do it tomorrow," "I'll do it next week," I'll do it next year, "I'll do," "I'll do," "I'll do?" We "I'll do." so much that it becomes our best friend. The phrase "I'll do" is the safety net that lets us off the hook from achieving our goals and convinces us there is a better time in the future.

I am not sure if you heard the news, if not, let me share it. EXTRA, EXTRA read all about it, the headline reads, "Tomorrow, Next Week, Next Year is not promised." As Les Brown stated, "The graveyard is the richest place on the earth, because it is here that you will find all the hopes and dreams that were never fulfilled, the books that were never written, songs that were never sung, inventions that were never shared, the cures that were never discovered, all because someone was too afraid to take the first step to carry out their dreams."

The richest place on this planet is the graveyard where people have left this earth and have not birthed their dreams due to this dream snatcher known as "Procrastination."

The crowd stood in amazement and went wild clapping in the wall to wall packed auditorium at my sixth-grade graduation. I was amazed myself because I had walked through the fire of fear and did what I never thought I would ever be asked to do and that's to give the keynote speech for my sixth-grade graduation class. You see, I wasn't the smartest kid in the class, I wasn't the kid that was chosefn to lead the annual school play. In fact, it was just the opposite; I remember always being picked to be in the plays but never the one in the lead role or what I would call a significant role. For example, in the play Cats, I remember it like yesterday, I was on the stairs saying meow with the other extras in the play. The role was needed, but it wasn't a significant role so how in the world did she pick me to give the sixth-grade graduation speech? I often wondered whether it was punishment for always getting myself and those that sat near me in trouble because I loved talking and laughing? Thinking back as an adult, I realized my teacher saw something in me that I didn't see in myself and that's the gift of speech. It was from that moment when I witnessed first-hand how I impacted those students and parents with my motivational speech written by my aunt Doris Stene, that left me with a burning passion for speaking and inspiring people.

Initially my major in college initially was in communication because I enjoyed speaking. My goal was to be a news reporter, anchor woman and eventually get my own TV Talk Show like the woman I admired, Oprah Winfrey. I abandoned my dream after speaking with my father and being advised that computer science offered more job opportunities and society was trending in the technology direction. I took Dad's advice because he was great at researching and provided me with all the data around the number of jobs available. He knew I loved math, so it seemed to be a good fit. I may have abandoned the communications field, but I never lost the love of speaking.

As they say, you know you love something when you can do it for free, and I freely spoke for my sorority and other organizations because I have a love and passion for helping people. While I was working at a very well-known computer company in Texas, I signed up and joined the internal toastmaster organization, and I learned people were making an excellent living speaking and helping people which reignited my passion and gave me that yearning to want to pursue a livelihood speaking.

I then met a co-worker who shared my passion for speaking, and he developed a plan, got laser focused and put the plan in action. I attended his first engagement to support him but also to inspire myself to have the courage to pursue my dream of speaking. I put off pursuing my dream of speaking as he continued his journey.

Today he is walking in his destiny and running a very successful speaking company and teaching others how they can do the same. See when you put things off, the dream killer procrastination has a way of coming full-circle and slapping you in the head for not acting.

Twenty years later my co-worker who didn't allow procrastination to stop him is now my coach. If you're like me and can relate to this story, you have permitted procrastination to have the last say-so for far too long.

The longer you put off achieving the goals that are important to you it starts to lose the value it once held in your life. You begin to question your goals and dreams, second guessing because if you have gone this long without it, do you really need to stretch yourself to reach this goal? You look up three, six, nine or twenty years from now in the same position with your goals sitting on the "I'll do" mantle. Don't be one of them; start today even if it's taking small steps to do something to move you towards achieving whatever goal you have set for yourself. The antidote for procrastination is action, action, and just in case you missed it, action.

I hope you decide like I did this year to no longer allow this dream killer to prohibit you from achieving any more of your goals no matter what. I had the dream of writing this book ten years ago, after working with my clients and mentees helping them develop in their professional careers and win.

I finally wrote this book because I broke the marriage vows to procrastination and married myself, vowing always to pursue my dreams. So, whether I succeed or fail, I can tell you one thing, I will pursue all my goals, I may do it with teeth chattering and knees knocking as my coach says, but I will no longer allow procrastination to win.

Perceived Lack of Knowledge, we have heard the saying, "Knowledge is Power." This saying keeps us continually seeking to learn more and aid in our being the information junkies that we are today. Due to this, we inhale knowledge from newspapers, courses, social media, television, anywhere we can locate new information. I am a proponent for continuously learning and growing your skills, a leader never stops learning; however, I am not an advocate for you leveraging this as an excuse to remain stuck.

We do not lack the knowledge to get started on our journey to where we want to be, but we are missing a critical component to why we are stuck, and that is failing to act on the knowledge that we already have learned. Motivational Speaker Tony Robbins says, "Knowledge is not Power. Knowledge is only potential Power. Action is Power." Knowledge is potential power because knowledge alone will not get us unstuck and moving towards transformation. I even challenge Tony Robbins statement and say,

"Knowledge or Action alone is not Power. Knowledge in Action is Power." You need both Knowledge and Action together to generate the electrons that produce the Power.

Recently I watched the classic movie "Rocky," and his boxing trainer was training him to "Stick and Move" because when he hits his opponent, the reflex is for the opponent to punch back and if he doesn't move he is likely to get knocked out. I urge you to do like Rocky. We must be boxers for our careers. When we hit the books, seminars, workshops and gain all this knowledge I say, "Learn and Act," like in the movie "Rocky" because the learning is the "Stick," and acting is the "Move." If you are learning and not applying or acting on that knowledge, you are losing to your opponent which in the corporate world is your fellow coworkers who are asking and applying for the same raise or promotion.

There are times where we cannot move forward because we don't have the adequate knowledge. In this case, you want to quickly gain the knowledge that aligns with your goals and the next opportunity you want to pursue. Whether it's learning how to work cross-functionally with other organizations, learning how to lead and mentor others or working effectively with global teams, you must plan to learn it now. Leaders are not born, they are developed and every skillset can be learned.

Whether you are leading your projects or leading other people, you're a leader and leaders never stop learning. You may not be pursuing a degree or certificate, but there are always free classes you can attend at work or online. You can learn anything you want to learn. There are no excuses why we cannot be continuously learning and growing.

If what you're learning is not going to be leveraged this year, then prioritize it in your training plan closer to the timeframe you will use it. This way you don't lose the knowledge, and you are not putting the precious time in the wrong area. Developing your training plan will give you more time to gain the experience in the essential high priority learning areas.

My client Valorie was beyond frustrated, she felt stuck, and opportunities just were not an option for her because she had been in her current job at the same level for ten years. Yes, like most she was getting the standard annual cost of living raises, but her career was not moving forward, and she was always being overlooked for promotions. Valorie had earned several degrees in which her company funded which further frustrated her because she was making all the right moves to obtain the education but was not seeing the fruits of her labor.

I know we can all relate to a time in our career when we were being overlooked and not recognized for our knowledge and hard work. Year after year she continued not to be considered for job opportunities; this caused her to start doubting and discounting her education and continuously seeking out ways to gain more knowledge. As I sat back and analyzed her current situation, I was having a hard time pinpointing where she lacked the knowledge. At the time, she had more education than her manager that was leading her department. I scheduled mentoring sessions with her and we spent multiple hours brainstorming and mapping her knowledge to several role responsibilities. What we discovered during this process was what she thought she was missing in knowledge, she already knew to receive the raise or promotion she desired.

Then it hit me—my favorite childhood motivational song, "Whistle While You Work." This Snow-White Disney song motivated me back in the day when I need to get moving on my house chores. The song says, "It won't take long if we sing along and whistle while we work." I leverage this song in my head when I need to get going on a task and I feel like I cannot move forward without having all the details. Another impactful part of the song says, "When there's too much to do, don't let it bother you, come on get smart, tune up and start and whistle while you work." I coached Valorie on the importance of continuing to learn as each of us should because leaders are learners and learning leads to more significant earnings.

Then we put together a plan that helped her prioritize her training plan so it's not just something else to do. I strongly encouraged her to gain the knowledge with a plan about ways to apply it so that you're acting and doing as the song suggests, "Whistle While You Work."

Effective Communication is the key to getting anything we want to happen in our life. If we are going to spend time communicating, we should ensure it has the impact we need to move us forward. There are three forms of communication that we must master:

1) Verbal
2) Nonverbal
3) Written

All forms of communication have their place, and it's critical we learn how to effectively leverage them to gain credibility and trust with the valuable people in our organizations.

Communication should be done in a way that it is clear, concise, powerful and quick; you want the person you're conversing with to be actively listening and able to absorb and understand what you're trying to say to them.

In our careers and life, we stay stuck because we have not mastered this skill of communication. Let's address verbal communication; I thought my hard work would speak for me and showcase my desires of wanting more for my career. Help me say, "Wrong!" When was the last time you heard hard work talking? I had to tell myself, the work can't speak, but I can speak on its behalf. It's your responsibility to convey to your managers what you have accomplished and why the skills you have gained along the way have positioned you to deserve a strategic project, to work cross-functionally with other organizations or to serve on a higher level.

During my fight to get the performance improvement plan "PIP" revoked, I came to grips with this fact: I needed to own the message behind what gets communicated up to my leadership team. My director had no idea of the magnitude of what I was managing or the successful launches as a result of my commitment and hard work.

Our managers time is divided due to the many demands that come along with leading large, diverse teams as well as managing their own careers. We are doing our careers and self a disservice if we are not documenting and communicating regularly our accomplishments.

It is high risk to leave this task up to our boss, and I guarantee you some accomplishments will be missed or misunderstood. Communicating our accomplishments humbly and gracefully is our responsibility.

There is nothing wrong with celebrating your successes (aka tooting your horn). I say toot your horn and toot it often; it does not serve you to water down your achievements so that others feel secure around you.

The good book says, "You have not, because you ask not." Start communicating and asking for what you want then watch how your life will change. Statistics show that promotions come more frequently to employees who can communicate effectively.

Emotional Intelligence is your ability to do the following successfully:
1) Identify and manage your own emotions

2) Pick-up on the emotions of others

3) Build trust, credibility and grow influence

If we fail to master our emotions, it can cause us to stay stuck. I allowed my feelings to show on my sleeve whenever someone would do things that didn't align with how I thought things should happen or if I sensed they were trying to sabotage me or my career.

It is not wise to allow someone's bad behavior to control how you react to a situation. Being loud, boisterous, and pushy may get you some attention, but it certainly does not get you respect. Charles R. Swindoll, Author of Grace Awakening, said, "Life is 10% of what happens to us and 90% of how we react to it."

If we allow people to control our emotions, they will control our paycheck. Michelle Obama said it best, "When they go low, we go high." While investing the time to rise in our organizations, we should equally invest the time learning how to stay there by controlling and managing our emotions. People do not care how much you know if they don't want to work with you; guard your emotions.

Quick Tips: Breaking Mental Barriers

1) Embrace Fear: fall in love with fear and do it anyway. Great things are accomplished leveraging the power of fear.
2) Be Assertive and not Aggressive: Remove the emotion and speak from a position of hard data (aka facts)
3) Prioritize and Do It: Action is the antidote to break procrastination, complete high priority task first, don't put off for tomorrow what you can do today, tomorrow may never come, and if it does most times it comes with a new set of tasks, it's called life.
4) Actively listen: This is the best form of communication. Listening helps you understand the person's perspective and you can tailor your message to meet their needs.

Chapter 2: Raise Your Visibility

"Why allow your Greatness to be boxed in, when you were born to Stand Out?"
—Karyn Quick

One of the biggest misconceptions in the workplace today is that we will be noticed working hard in our cubes and will be rewarded for all our hard work. I am here to dispel this myth, there is much more to this story and working hard is just one piece of the puzzle. Another major part is standing up, standing out, and being visible in your organization.

According to an article in Careershifters, "Why the Best Jobs are never advertised and How to find them", 70% of jobs are never advertised. What this means ladies is majority of the jobs never make it to the job board. We must get beyond the cubes and raise our visibility so that we are strategically positioning ourselves to win.

It was October 2006, excited and grateful were two of the feelings I felt as I plowed through an ocean of snow, due to a blizzard that had hit the Midwest, heading into the office to start my new job. Although filled with excitement, I didn't expect the first day back to be met with Jack Frost and his cousin Chicago Hawk.

They say everything big in Texas, everything except these big bad winter storms that rage through the Midwest. When that Chicago Hawk hit me from behind, I was contemplating heading right back to Texas. I thought to myself, "I see why they call it the 'Hawk;' that wind sneaks up on you and cuts deep just like a real 'Hawk' as they sneak upon and devour their prey."

Despite the frigid weather, I was elated to be starting my new job with a well-respected Pharma company and to be only a few hours from my hometown in Michigan.

Shortly after beginning my new job there was a mandatory meeting called to discuss a program that the IT CIO was rolling out to the organization. The new program was to be a blueprint for the way IT professionals were to engage and work. The presentation was exciting as the team members articulated the value and impact the program would have on our environment to shape the culture. Upon completing the presentation, the last slide highlighted the team members, as I scanned the slide and questioned myself, "How can this be a program to shape the organization, yet it didn't represent a population that could offer diverse perspectives?" Without hesitation, I quickly raised my hand and asked how the team was formed, and I was faced with a question that landed on me like a ton of bricks.

I was asked, "Would you like to be on the team?" This was a pivotal point for me and several thoughts went through my mind. At first, I thought, "I am way too busy to take on another job." The team conveyed they would frequently be meeting onsite and offsite to discuss and develop the program. Secondly, I thought, "Would this be worth the investment of my time?" I was new to this organization, so I had another talk with myself; I said, "Self this is a great way to engage and serve your new organization on a higher level by participating in a program that was being driven by senior leadership."

This opportunity allowed me to give freely of my time and talents which resulted in me being in the space of valuable people whom I would not have interacted with on a daily basis. I was able to learn from them, as well as share my own knowledge and experience which gave them the opportunity to experience first-hand the value I brought to the organization. This was a strategic move for me because now I was associated with something positive in their minds. I learned when you help people achieve a goal that is important to them you instantly become liked and you win favor with them.

I know if I had not made this sacrifice and moved differently, I would not have had the opportunity to meet the various leaders and change agents at the speed I was able to meet them. This decision had such a profound impact that I had become the "Go-To" person for questions only after being at the company for a few months. One of my co-workers said, "Ask Karyn; she has been here several years."

She almost had me convinced I worked there longer, then I shocked her and myself when I told her I had only been at the company three months.

It's about strategic positioning. You must insert yourself in the right situation in order to gain exposure with the right people. The traditional approach of being visible by simply attending the town hall meetings, webinars, lunch and learns, are not designed to invoke effective interaction with valuable people.

My client Clare was laid off from her job, and she began contracting for this Fortune 500 company. Feeling frustrated and down, she called me to vent and discuss why she had not been offered a full-time position as her contract position was being extended once again for the second year.

During our conversation, one thing becomes clear. Clare neglected to let her boss know that she desired to be a full-time employee. She didn't have scheduled weekly meetings with her boss, and she barely saw him.

Clare was a shy person and speaking up and being visible did not come naturally for her; she struggled with being in the forefront. As her coach, one piece of advice I gave her was to think of ways to connect with her Boss outside her cube. Connecting with her boss outside the cube would allow her to engage with him and get to know him on a deeper level. Then she could also share with him during their conversation how she was contributing to the success of his team.

There were many contractors reporting to her boss. What would set her apart to be viewed as someone to hire instead of the other contractors on the same team?

There was another complexity added into the mix. Clare was shy and didn't have the confidence to speak up on her behalf so in this case I had her seek out quality people she could leverage to speak on her behalf. Because I had built a relationship with her boss, she chose me to speak on her behalf and make the connection so that she could start the process of positioning herself to be considered for a role on his team. The connection was made, and within six months Clare had received a full-time position with the company.

To truly raise your visibility, you must differentiate yourself. As the saying goes, "It's crowded at the bottom." In Clare's case, she was just one of many contractors that had a desire to be hired full-time.

Developing a strategy that will set you apart and position you for success is the goal. The strategy should address two major components: "Strategic Position" and "Strategic Action."

Following are the key areas to focus on as you devise your plan:

Strategic Position:
1) Sustainable Competitive Advantage
2) Identify Your Unique Value Proposition
3) Build and Maintain Solid Brand
4) Have a Core Marketing Message

5) Position Yourself to be Visible

Strategic Action:
1) Cause a Disruption; Amaze/Wow them
2) Communicate your Differentiated advantage
3) Highlight Specific Skillsets
4) Create Buzz - Attention for your Achievements
5) Be Remarkably You

Be willing to stand out from amongst the crowd and take a different approach which may mean traveling down a road less travelled or if there is not a path, creating it and being willing to fail to learn the lessons that will propel you forward.

To have a competitive advantage, you want to position yourself to be memorable and not just merely seen. A visible employee who is remembered for her contribution and value, has a competitive advantage over one who is seen galloping from event to event.

Be the change you want to see. The late Michael Jackson said, "It starts with the Man in the Mirror" and I say, "It starts with the Woman in the Mirror". Investing time in you to differentiate yourself makes your brand stand out from the others. Many shy away from being visible and would rather stick with the status quo or sit in the seat of mediocrity because it's comfortable.

Being visible comes with a cost and I would be lying if I told you otherwise. There is a cost of being uncomfortable, cost of time, cost of sleep and it may cost your financially depending on the situation; I am sure there may be some additional costs that I missed.

As Transformational Coach Lisa Nichols says, "Your Conviction and Convenience don't live on the same block."

Transforming will never be convenient; there is nothing in life worth having that doesn't require commitment and sacrifice.

Although there is a price, here are some of the 'Pros' of being visible:
1) You Become Unstoppable
2) You Develop Your Voice
3) You feel Empowered and Energized
4) You Gain Credibility and Trust
5) You Self-promote

When I decided to get out of my own way and stand out to become visible in order to prove myself as a viable asset, it was the best investment I could have made for my career development and growth.

Quick Tips to Raising Your Visibility:

1) Identify and Join Professional Organizations: Seek those with senior leadership support. Be involved and serve from a leadership position whenever possible, whether you're the lead or a committee member. (i.e. Toast Masters, Women's Leadership Groups)

2) Develop a Differentiation Strategy: What is your competitive advantage, unique value or core marketing message for yourself?

3) Seek out Strategic projects: These projects are more visible and usually align with senior leaders or your company's annual goals.

4) Project Professionalism: Remember; "Your Image is You." Be mindful of

how you dress, talk and conduct yourself during work hours and while attending after hour functions.

Chapter 3: Boost Your Brand

"Branding is the lifeline to your being. We are CEOs of our own companies, "Me Inc." Our most important job is to be the head marketer for the brand called "You."
— Karyn Quick

A roaring round of applause filled the room as I reported the TechGyrls were confirmed and mentors assigned to the girls. Wrapping up my report and reviewing the volunteer schedule, I heard a voice lean in and say, "I would like to mentor you."

Delighted, I turned around to see who had uttered the statement; to my surprise, it was one of the top female IT Directors. I was shocked that such a time had come in my career where I was not seeking mentorship, mentorship found me.

During our first meeting, the mentor asked, "Have you wondered why I asked to mentor you?"

I replied, "The thought did cross my mind; can you please elaborate?"

She informed me that she had been watching my interaction, leadership skills, engagement and saw me as a person who could be a vital part of the leadership team serving in a higher role and she wanted to mentor me in getting to the next level.

Being mentored excited me because I knew this relationship could lead to more significant opportunities for me. I had a senior leader who would be committed to helping me achieve my goals as long as I stayed committed. The light bulb in my head brightened as I thought back. This leader saw the value in my engaging on committees and raising my hand to lead.

I remember back when I was trying to become visible to build and boost my brand; I sought out organizations I could join that had senior leadership support, like Toastmasters, Women groups and other IT organizations. It was not the joining alone that made a difference for me, it was the serving that set me apart. Most time when we try to build our brand within our organization, we approach it from a position of what we are going to gain versus how we can be of service.

I went in with a service attitude, and in the serving, I built strong relationships and was able to showcase my brand. Due to my interaction and involvement, I was also able to gain knowledge and skills in a non-threatening environment with top leaders in the organization. These leaders were people I probably would not have connected with while working my typical day to day job.

Through this engagement, I was asked by one of the top Directors to mentor me which lead into my securing a position within her organization without even having to interview for the job. This is the power of offering your service and boosting your brand.

In building and boosting my brand over the last twenty years, one of the tools I remember leveraging was the "P.I.E.' tool.

Embracing your piece of the "P.I.E" is important. Let's explore the definition of "PIE."

- **Performance (P)** – Performance is how you start the branding engine. You perform and it's the catalyst to jumpstarting all other aspects of your career. Alone, it is rarely sufficient.

- **Image (I)** – Your reputation proceeds you; consider these questions while building or strengthening your brand: "How will I be remembered when I am not in the room? What will people say about me?"

- **Exposure (E)** – This speaks to your participation and relevancy in an organization. Spend time exploring these questions; "Who knows Me? Who has my back? and "Who Cares?" Have you taken the time to become visible and show yourself as a viable asset?

How you show-up on your job is how you will be remembered; first impressions are lasting. Protect your brand as it is the roadmap for how people will relate to you, respect you and value your knowledge. Your image is in direct correlation with building or destroying your brand. Your brand is who you are, what you stand for and how you will connect and interact with valuable people.

Branding yourself at work is where Documentation meets Conversation. You see I became very good at documentation thanks to one of my mentors who taught me it only holds weight if its documented. Where I struggled like most Women is in the sharing and ensuring everyone had visibility and was aware of my brand because I didn't want to come off as boastful, arrogant and self-centered.

Having a solid brand is the heartbeat to a successful, thriving career. Personal branding builds up your reputation to the point where you have a presence even when you're not present.

Quick Tips to Boosting Your Brand:

1) Embrace your "PIE": Gain clarity on how you will leverage each area for brand positioning.
2) Maintain High Integrity: Your word is your bound, say what you mean and follow through on what you say.
3) Stand Out: Don't be afraid of Leading and being out front. Have the conversations to ensure everyone knows your brand and what you stand for.
4) Guard Social Media: Be cautious of your connections and how you show-up online.

Chapter 4: Connection is Collection: It's Who Knows You and Your Value

"It's not who you know, but who knows you and knows you for the value that you bring to the organization."

—Karyn Quick

"Model Successful People, there is nothing wrong with being a copy-cat as long as you copy the right cat."

—Karyn Quick

"Surround yourself with Only Quality People (OQP)."

—Les Brown

It's not empowering alone for you to know who the valuable people or change agents are in your organization. What I have seen during my 25 years in Corporate America is that people go around name dropping various top leaders' names because they think it's impressive and that it sends a message that they are connected on a much higher level. However, these are the same people I have witnessed standing around in the breakrooms complaining about how dissatisfied they are with their jobs and how frustrated they are because they are not moving forward in their career.

What I have found to be most impactful and impressive is when people recognize who you are, understand and appreciate the value you bring to the organization. This type of connection I want you to work on developing for yourself because this is a real connection that will move the needle in getting you closer to your goals and you will start seeing the change in your career.

Building your value proposition so that people know you and the value you bring is a two-part process. The first part is having self-awareness of the value you bring to an organization. Why is it important to know your value? These are a few reasons why knowing your value is essential:

1) Liberating
2) Empowering
3) Unstoppable

Liberating because you are now consciously aware of your value and know you have it in you to succeed no matter the cost.

Empowering because you have unlocked the door to your greatness and can stand on the values you possess.

Unstoppable because you gain the confidence to share amongst people who can change the trajectory of your career.

You have identified your value, now what? The second part is to connect and communicate the value with the valuable people you have determined that you want to meet because they align with your 2-yr, 3-yr or 5-yr plan you have set for yourself. It's important to position yourself amongst key leaders in your organization, so they get to know you on a deeper level.

Here are some questions you can ask yourself: Does your Director know your name? Does your VP know your name? Do Cross Functional Leaders, those that may not necessarily be in your organization, know your name? If they know your name, give yourself a round of applause because that is the first step and an essential part of building a relationship and connecting with leaders.

Now ask yourself these set of questions: Do these leaders know the value you bring? Do these leaders see the ROI (Return on Investment) they are getting by having you there? If you answered no to any of these questions, it's a problem, and we must get you out of your cubes and adding more value to valuable people. As the good books say, "Seek and ye shall find." We must get out of self-limiting beliefs, doubts and fears that are holding us back from seeking out and then reaching out to build the relationships that will make the difference.

The embarrassment, betrayal, and disrespect I felt upon being placed on a performance improvement plan (PIP) left me vowing never to allow myself to be in a position where I wasn't known for the value that I brought to an organization by more than just my immediate manager and organization. After countless hours of pondering the thought of how I would do this, the tool of choice that stood out for me was "Networking." The Networking term can be overly used but don't be fooled, it is still an essential tool that bridges the gap between the haves and the have-nots.

Networking is best described as developing a mutually beneficial relationship for interpersonal interaction, and smart women understand the importance of building and nurturing their relationships.

I just got to work, I booted up my computer, and I noticed my company was spotlighting one of the top leaders for the impact she was making in the organization through her work and volunteer efforts. It intrigued me to want to know more about this individual, so I scurried to get my pen to note her name. Quickly I pulled up her name on the intranet, then I set the plan in motion to reach out to ask her if we could meet for lunch.

I was new to the company, and the sooner I connected and met valuable people the better. I reached out, and she agreed to have lunch with me. During the conversation, to my surprise, we had a lot in common that extended beyond work. I found out she served on non-profit boards as I did and that she participated in community service as I did in my organization.

It's important you ask the right strategic questions to get to know the valuable person, but it is equally important to expand your conversation when possible beyond work, so you can further explore where you might connect with a valuable person in other areas of their life.

The more you can connect the stronger the bound and it's easier to cultivate the new relationship. I made a conscious decision to connect to start the process of being known in the company.

Quick Tips to Connecting and Collecting:

1) Determine your Value: Think in terms of results you produce and not tasks you perform; make them memorable because you want to leave that "WOW" factor.

2) Document your Value: Documentation solidifies your Value: People believe if it's important enough to document it must be valuable information. Remember, "Documentation Beats Conversation."

3) Share your Value: It's not boosting and bragging to speak up about your contributions. This sends a message to valuable people in your organization that

you're ready to go to that next level or assume more responsibilities.

Chapter 5: Get Started: Life is Waiting

"It's not when you start, it's that you start and don't stop until you win!"
—Karyn Quick

As I sat working through lunch in my cube on a sizzling hot summer Texas day, it must have been close to 100 degrees that day, my boss rushed down the hall headed towards my cube. Excitedly he handed me an award for my anniversary with the company. In my mind, it was bitter-sweet; sweet because it was nice to have been successful in working for the company, bitter that I was nowhere near where I thought I would be after eight years in my career. You see I had a goal of being a director one day, yet I was still in a non-managerial role. I realize the dream was big, but why spend time dreaming if you're not going to dream BIG. As the saying goes, "If your dream doesn't scare you it is not big enough." I had truly picked a dream that scared me to the point of where I spent nights tossing and turning thinking of how I was going to accomplish my goal. While working in IT early on in my career I wasn't seeing any women hired into director roles, as I went on in my career I started to see a few women achieving this position, but none of the women looked like me. I doubted myself and I instantly felt defeated and put what I thought at the time was "a pie in the sky" dream on the back burner. I compromised what I wanted to achieve because I didn't think it could ever happen for me.

I want you to take a moment and ask yourself, "What are you compromising daily by not taking the actions necessary to move you from where you are today to where you want to be?"

What I didn't consider at the time was by me compromising what I really wanted and not being willing to act to pursue my dream despite what it looked like on the outside, caused me delaying some big goals I had for myself for twenty years. Looking back over the years, now I know I should have taken the risk and did it anyway. I was missing the big picture and slowly dimming the light on my greatness and the value I brought to the organization. It is true what a man thinketh so is he, so if you think you can't, you're right, but if you think you can, guess what? You will find a way to make it happen no matter what!

I can tell you I compromised my desire to pursue my dream of being a speaker and coach to empower and uplift women. My goal and passion are to help women overcome many of the barriers that kept me stuck in my career, so they would have the support that I didn't have to move forward sooner, quicker and faster.

I know what I have could help another woman overcome resistance, but, instead I sat down and didn't act toward fulfilling my dream. Instead of having the confidence to push past my limiting belief I succumbed to it and did my job and didn't look for opportunities or ways to reverse the status quo or break down the perceived glass ceilings. I now know what was holding me back and what kept me stuck in a non-leadership role for eight years and not pursuing my dream to start my speaking business for twenty years was my fear of failure. I paused my dream for way too many years; what dreams are you pausing? Is it not going after the job you know you desire and deserve? Is it not requesting the raise that could allow you to save money to support your children's college education fund so that you free them from the burden of student loans? Is it continuing to work for a company or a boss that doesn't appreciate or respect you for the value you bring? Is it accepting and settling for the eighty cents to every dollar your male counterpart makes for performing the same job because something is better than nothing? Is it being fine with your co-workers being promoted over you, knowing you trained them to do the job they are doing so well?

As I think back on my career, there are times I wish I had the tenacity and confidence to take calculative risks and was more proactive in pursuing some of my goals so that I could have moved forward sooner, faster and quicker. I wish I would have made it okay to fail versus failing by default playing it safe.

My client Maria also had the same struggle with taking risks as well, and when I started mentoring and coaching her, she was beyond frustrated due to the lack of progress she had made in her career. She had achieved her degree while working full-time in manufacturing but still was stuck in the same mundane job for twelve years.

The learnings from the failures as well as successes have allowed me to develop and grow. I still believe that if I had moved forward sooner It would have allowed me to impact more women that came behind me.

My co-worker Sherrell scheduled a one on one meeting with me for what I thought was our typical meeting where she would leverage me to advise her on different scenarios of how to be effective in her job. I walked into the meeting and saw Sherrell bent over crying hysterically and she looked up with this look of devastation. Stunned I didn't know what to say so I stood there, and she eventually stated that her son was accepted into the college of his dreams. Puzzled I was wondering, okay, I know kids go away to college all the time; it can't be this bad.

Then she proceeded to say the college gave him a scholarship, but it wouldn't be enough to cover the entire tuition, room and board. This was the college he always dreamed of attending, yet due to lack of funds and due to living paycheck to paycheck, Sherrell was not able to put up money for a college fund.

The son was excelling and had high grades, but the school required more tuition than even the good grades could secure for him. It devastated her to think her hands were tied and that she would have to inform her son that he couldn't attend the college of his dreams. She blamed her willingness to stay comfortable and not to go after her dreams was having a downhill impact on her ability to help her son fulfill his dream.

She told herself at that moment to no longer play it safe and to go after her dreams. She immediately scheduled a meeting with me and we mapped out a plan of where she was in her career to where she wanted to be, and I helped her strategically identify the gaps in her skillset for the career she wanted to pursue.

Together we mapped out the skills she needed to acquire, resources she needed to help her acquire those skills and the valuable people she needed to connect with to help her navigate and seek out opportunities and I would be an advocate for her.

My client no longer put her dreams on hold, acted on her plan that day and has never looked back. Today she is a Director for a large tech company and now she is able to help her son pay off his college tuition debt so when he finishes college, he can begin his career debt free.

Conclusion

Women! Hold your heads high; you have the knowledge and tenacity in you now to start implementing these quick tips to move your career forward.

Get started pursuing your dreams, don't allow your self-limiting beliefs to have you doubting your abilities and keep you from getting started. It's not when you start; it's that you start and don't stop until you win. Start with making the small needlepoint moves, this will build your confidence and show you that it's possible to achieve your goals.

The stories highlighted in this book have shown you that you are not running this race alone; I hope they left you feeling motivated and inspired to get started. There have been many women that have paved the roads for us so that we could make it this far. There are those women who are waiting and watching what we are going to do so that they can see it's possible and know that if it's possible for us they can see themselves doing it as well. If not for yourself, think of all the women who are coming behind you that you will mentor either directly or indirectly by your actions.

Show them it's possible and lead them to shout loud, "I'm Possible!"

My greatest hope for you reading this book is that you will be able to move forward and achieve great things in your career without external or internal challenges slowing you down or making you second guess your strengths, abilities and goals.

Smart women move differently, and I want you to make the quick moves, break down all barriers, climb higher and expand your scope; your success will help to make your organization, your family and ultimately the world a better place.

Smart Women Keep The Conversation Going…

My goal for this book is not the end of our conversation but to be the catalyst to starting a great movement with "Smart Women."

Let's continue our discussions by joining the Audacious Women Excelling Community at fb.me/AudaciousWomenExcelling.

This community is designed for women to support and learn from each other while we continue to work through the challenges mentioned in the book. In this community, we will explore those topics that are critical to your success. Women and men are all welcome to join.

Visit my website to book me for Speeches, Women Retreats, Conferences, Graduations and other events: www.Quick6Wins.com.

On the cover, I offered a free coaching session; book your ten-minute call by sending me an email at KQuick@TheQuick6Wins.com and write 'Cubeonomic Free Coaching Session' in the subject line.

www.ingramcontent.com/pod-product-compliance
Lightning Source LLC
Chambersburg PA
CBHW071410220526
45469CB00004B/1243